Sally Ride
Science

W9-CLZ-488

3/10

John Johnson, Jr.

LIVING GREEN

Rb.
Flash Point

ROARING BROOK PRESS

NEW YORK

Living
Green

000000011111111111111111110000000000000000000000001111110000000111111110000011111111110000000000 111111111 000

CONTENTS

1

HOPES AND HURDLES

Planet Earth is big and heavy. It sure seems like it goes about the business of being a planet without regard for us small humans. The truth is, though, that our world is the way it is because of a delicate balance between plants, animals, microbes, water, land, air, and . . . us.

We humans are rightly proud of what we've achieved. We've created farming methods that feed billions of people. We've invented cars, trains, and planes. We've developed technologies that have illuminated the night, and brought music, TV, and the Internet into billions of homes.

But our successes have not come without consequences. We've upset the balance. Increasingly, our activities—from heating our homes to increasing the yields on our farms to making fast food even faster—have affected the precious resources on which we depend for our very lives.

[2] WHAT'S ALL THE FUSS ABOUT?

Before around 1750 people didn't have much of an effect on Earth. And for good reason. There weren't many of us on the planet—fewer than 1 billion. Since then, the number of people has skyrocketed. Today, there are over 6.5 billion of us. With more and more people on the planet, there are more and more changes to our air, water, and land.

What Goes Around . . .

The air we breathe has become increasingly polluted. Smog, which once seemed a problem only in big cities such as Los Angeles and Pittsburgh, has spread around the world. As the economies of developing nations have boomed, so has the output of pollution. In Beijing, China, it's so smoggy that Chinese leaders ordered cutbacks in industry and car emissions for the 2008 Olympic games.

In some places, like Mexico City, the smog is so bad people seldom see a blue sky.

Overworked Water

We humans are pretty smart. Thousands of years ago, we learned we could use water to help make our lives easier. Early farmers planted their crops in a way that channeled rain into their fields. Then they learned to dig wells. Finally, they learned to use the energy in flowing water to make electricity at giant dams. Today, though, we're making our water work too hard. We're using too much water to keep our lawns and cities green, especially in desert areas. And we're dumping waste into our rivers. In many parts of the world, the water is so polluted it's not fit to drink. We're smart, so why are we acting so dumb?

The Three Gorges Dam in China lets loose water to lower the level in the reservoir behind it.

This Land is *Not* Your Land

We're all familiar with the way we've changed the landscape. You can see the results every day—new roads, new homes, new shopping malls cut into the countryside. More than 6.5 billion people live on our planet. And every one of us needs food, water, clothing, and shelter. This is driving megachanges to our forests, farmlands, and waterways.

A huge swath of tropical rainforest in Borneo was cut down to make way for a palm oil plantation.

7

Our Changing Climate

All these changes add up to something even bigger. It's called climate change. And it means that all over the world, Earth's climate is changing—it's getting warmer. So far, most of the effects have been small. But scientists agree there's big trouble ahead—melting ice caps, rising sea levels, more and worse droughts, and wildlife having to forage farther for food.

You Know What a Greenhouse Is, Right?

It's a warm place that lets in plenty of sunlight, but doesn't let much heat out. That describes what is happening to our Earth as certain molecules, primarily carbon dioxide, build up in the atmosphere. It's called the greenhouse effect.

Temperatures Rising

There are actually two kinds of greenhouse effects. One is natural, and it's good. It makes Earth warm enough for living things to be comfy—not too hot, not too cold. If the atmosphere did not absorb some of the Sun's rays and the heat reflected from Earth's surface, the world would be too cold for life. But if the greenhouse effect gets too big—if too much carbon dioxide and other gases that absorb radiation accumulate in the atmosphere— temperatures rise. That's what's happening now. And it's *not* good.

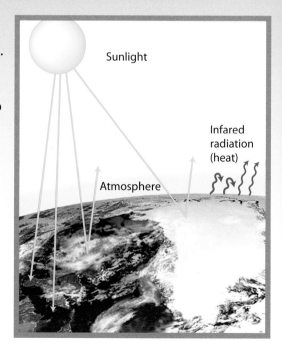

Sunlight

Infared radiation (heat)

Atmosphere

As carbon dioxide and other greenhouse gases from car and factory fumes build up in the air, our planet is getting warmer and warmer.

Pulse of Our Planet

The first prediction of climate change was made in 1896, by a Swedish chemist Svante Arrhenius. He saw that the Industrial Revolution would release large amounts of carbon dioxide into the air. Arrhenius predicted that if atmospheric carbon dioxide doubled, Earth would get several degrees warmer. Instruments all over the world, and in space, have now detected this temperature rise. Computer models show the buildup of carbon dioxide in the air will continue to increase in the future, as the economies of China and India grow and these heavily populated countries use more fossil fuels.

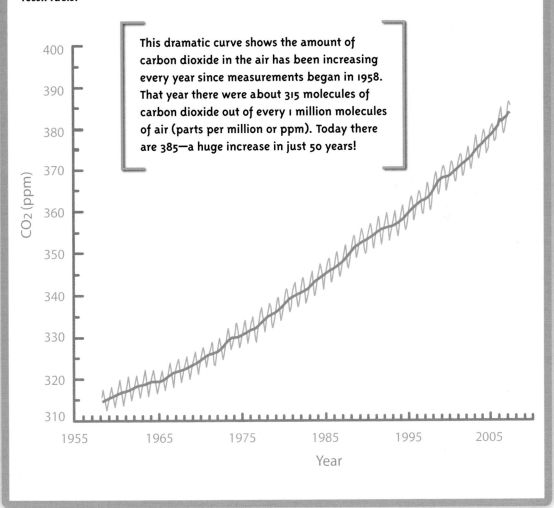

This dramatic curve shows the amount of carbon dioxide in the air has been increasing every year since measurements began in 1958. That year there were about 315 molecules of carbon dioxide out of every 1 million molecules of air (parts per million or ppm). Today there are 385—a huge increase in just 50 years!

Fill 'Er Up with Dino-fuel

Actually, it's not that simple. Scientists say that the oil used to make gasoline developed over many millions of years. Billions and trillions of small animals and plants decayed under layers of mud and water until only hydrogen and carbon were left. What about *T. rex?* There weren't enough dinosaurs around to make all the oil and other fossil fuels that we've been using for the past century.

2 Much CO_2

In one way, fossil fuels—oil, coal, and natural gas—are good fuel sources. A relatively small amount releases a lot of stored-up energy when it's burned. That's why coal was used for centuries to heat homes. Then people figured out how to refine oil to make gasoline, so it could be used to fuel automobiles. The trouble comes when lots of fossil fuels are burned by automobile engines and industrial plants all over the world. This releases carbon dioxide (CO_2), the same stuff you breathe out thousands of times a day. When over 6 billion people and 600 million cars, not to mention a couple of thousand power plants, are all pumping out carbon dioxide . . . well, you can see that's a lot.

Do the Write Thing

Are the folks on Capitol Hill tuned in to climate change? Try writing a letter to your congresswoman or congressman and find out. Tell her or him how you feel about climate change and ask what Congress is doing to address the problems we face. You may be surprised to know that members of Congress pay close attention to their mail. That's how they find out how people in their district feel about the issues that concern them.

Experts Tell Us — Frances Beinecke

President
Natural Resources Defense Council

Frances Beinecke runs an organization whose to-do list ranges from stopping global warming to protecting our oceans—and that's just for starters! As president of the Natural Resources Defense Council, Frances' job is to protect her "number one client: Planet Earth." While some would be overwhelmed, Frances isn't. "We made these problems, and we think we know how to solve them. The growing awareness and commitment to the environment that we're seeing is very, very positive." Frances works with lawmakers to put environmentally friendly policies in place, and then to make sure they're followed. She also challenges young people to get involved. "Are there places where your school could recycle more? How often do you carpool? How many energy-efficient appliances does your family use?" she asks. "Every person can make a tremendous difference, and everything starts at home by taking action."

The Good News

Yikes. So much bad news. Is there any hope? You betcha. There are solutions to every one of our problems. For example, in Los Angeles air quality has improved because pollution officials require industry and car manufacturers to cut smog. So the situation is far from hopeless. Some solutions are so simple you can do them today. Others will take time, and they will require help from our neighbors and friends.

[3] STEPS IN THE RIGHT DIRECTION

If we stop using so much fossil fuel, does that mean we'll all have to park our cars and start riding our bikes to school and work? Riding bikes does help. Unfortunately, there's no one, simple solution to the problem of replacing fossil fuels. But scientists around the world are working on clean energies. Some strange and exotic, others as simple as turning garbage into fuel.

Think, Think, Think

There are several ways to attack the problem. How about not using quite so much energy? Conservation is being practiced today almost everywhere in the U.S., and in many other places around the world, especially in Europe. Increasing the efficiency of our cars, boats, trains, and airplanes can help a lot. Less vroom, vroom.

Good Garbage

Landfills are like low-tech garbage disposals. In fact 65 percent of the trash dumped into them is made up of organic material such as banana peels, carrot tops, and potato skins. What a waste. Some researchers are studying the possibility of using all these veggies as fuel for a new generation of clean power plants.

What About Our Buddy, the Sun?

The largest solar power plant in the world is in California's Mojave Desert. It's actually nine solar plants spread across the sunbaked desert. What a sight! One million mirrors lined up in superlong rows move with the Sun, like sunflowers bending toward the light. Altogether, they produce enough energy to power nearly 80,000 homes in Southern California, with very little pollution. And there's no problem with safety. Too good to be true? Through current methods of generating power, only about 35 percent of the Sun's energy is converted into usable electricity. That means you need a lot of Sun to get not a lot of power. But its future is bright.

At Kramer Junction, long parabolic mirrors concentrate sunlight. This heats oil traveling through tubes. The superhot oil turns water into steam—the energy used to make electricity.

4 U 2 Do

Lasso the Sun's Energy

Check this out. Using a pop can, aluminum foil, and a rubber band, you can harness the Sun's energy. Wrap a piece of aluminum foil, shiny side up, over the bottom of the can. Keep the foil in place with the rubber band. Gently press the foil to smooth it out across the can bottom. Presto! You have a parabolic mirror. Now go outside and aim your mirror—the bottom of the can— toward the Sun. Slowly move a 2.5 centimeter x 7.5 centimeter (1 inch x 3 inch) strip of newspaper in front of the mirror. Observe what the reflected light from the mirror does on the paper. Do you see the focal point? What happens to the brightness when you pass the dark and light areas of the newspaper in front of it? Why? What do you think a megaparabolic mirror can do?

Check out your answers on page 38.

wind must be good for something besides messing up your hair. Good thought. A number of utility plants offer customers the chance to pay a little extra on their utility bills to buy wind-generated electricity. Wind power comes from giant windmills in mountain passes and other windy areas. There's got to be a catch, right? You're getting it. The problem with wind power, as with solar power, is inefficiency. It takes about 3.3 square meters (11 square feet) of land (about the size of a big bathroom) to generate enough power to turn on a light bulb. That's why wind farms have to be big—really big. Here comes a gust of wind. Hang onto your hat.

Our Friend, the Atom?

What about nuclear energy? Nuclear power plants are powered by uranium. One atom of uranium produces 10 million times more energy than one molecule of natural gas or oil or clump of coal. So nuclear power is an attractive alternative to fossil fuels. It also doesn't release greenhouse gases, so it's a clean energy source. Sounds great, right? But safety and storage of radioactive waste is risky business. Power plant accidents at Three Mile Island, Pennsylvania, and Chernobyl, in the former Soviet Union, threatened people and wildlife. The towns around Chernobyl are still uninhabitable—and the accident happened more than 20 years ago! Still nuclear power is a clean energy source, so engineers are working hard to make it safe.

Experts Tell Us

Sandra Begay-Campbell

Civil Engineer
Sandia National Laboratories

Most people take turning on a light for granted. Not Sandra Begay-Campbell. As a Native American who grew up outside a Navajo reservation in New Mexico, she knows firsthand that not every family has power lines near their homes. "The Navajo don't live in communities. They are scattered off by themselves, sometimes hundreds of miles across the desert," she says. As a civil engineer, Sandra works to bring alternative sources of energy, including solar and wind power, to Native Americans. Using renewable energy goes hand-in-hand with Native American philosophy. "Native Americans are very conscious of how they impact Earth and of doing what is necessary to keep it sustainable indefinitely for future citizens." Sandra loves the challenge of working with tribes, utilities, and homeowners to figure out how to install solar panels or wind turbines in remote places and make sure they're maintained in the future. "I like working with people and interacting with them to figure out all the pieces. Engineering is a very people-person job."

This Is Getting Frustrating

Now you're beginning to understand how hard it is to solve our energy problems. One thing we have going for us, though, is our imagination. It helped us become one of the most successful species on Earth. Now it's helping us figure out how to make a future that won't imperil our planet.

YOU WANT TO DO *WHAT?*

People all over the world are working on solutions to our environmental problems—especially global climate warming. Scientists and engineers are working on some pretty far-out and exciting ideas.

Being There

Anywhere but the Air

Some scientists think a good way to get rid of all the carbon dioxide is to bury it. It's called carbon sequestration. How do you bury a gas? Well, when you go deep enough under the ocean, around 3 kilometers (2 miles), the gas molecules get squeezed closer and closer together under all the pressure of the seawater above. The result: carbon dioxide becomes heavier than the water, so it stays put. Others are looking into the idea of putting it underground—in sandstone. A not-so-far-out idea . . . .

Norway's largest oil company buries 1 million metric tons (1 million tons) of carbon dioxide deep under the seafloor every year.

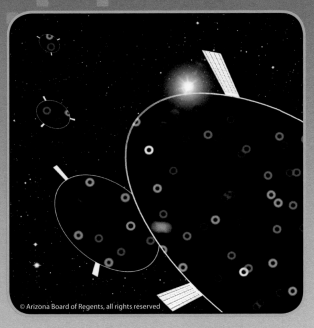

10 . . . 9 . . . 8 . . .

University of Arizona astronomer Roger Angel has proposed an idea that sounds as simple as holding up your hand to create a sunscreen. The plan would require launching thousands of little spaceships to form a giant shade tree between Earth and the Sun. The problem? It would take about 16 trillion little ships—20 million rocket launches—to form this space umbrella.

Each circle in this drawing is a tiny see-through spaceship made of clear plastic to deflect sunlight away from Earth. Each spaceship has three solar-reflecting tabs that direct its course.

Phytos to the Rescue

Fertilize the oceans? That's right. Iron is often rare in the ocean, yet it's a vital nutrient for phytoplankton—those tiny ocean plants that soak up carbon dioxide during photosynthesis. What if iron dust is tossed into the ocean so the little phytos multiply, or bloom, in the billions? Scientists and engineers wonder . . . if the blooms are big enough, could the phytoplankton suck up enough carbon dioxide to slow down global warming? Recently scientists from around the globe gathered at Woods Hole Oceanographic Institution to talk about the pros and cons of fertilizing the oceans with iron—and letting phytos come to our rescue.

Billions of phytoplankton add a milky green color to the water off the coast of South Africa.

17

[5] TRANSPORTATION INNOVATION

From trains to planes to automobiles, people are on the go. Fortunately, newer eco-friendly transportation technologies are on the move, too.

Thomas, the Efficient Tank Engine

Making trains more efficient is a global goal. In the U.S., railroad companies have invested in more fuel-efficient locomotives, as well as aluminum freight cars that weigh less and, therefore, use less fuel. Over a ten-year period, the energy used by freight trains dropped 16 percent. Computerized scheduling has also eliminated long idling times while trains wait for an open track. And now there is even a hybrid locomotive—just imagine a giant Prius rolling down the tracks. Choo, choo.

Being There

What's that UFO Doing on the Ground?

Solar-powered cars have been the dream of transportation companies for decades. Designers have made a lot of progress since the first models, which crawled along the highway and had to have wings like a jet to hold all the solar panels required to power the batteries. In 2007, the World Solar Challenge, a 3,021-kilometer (1,877-mile) race from Darwin to Adelaide, Australia, was won by *Nuna 4,* a car from the Netherlands. It averaged a stunning 103 kilometers (64 miles) an hour. The big drawback to solar-powered cars? You're grounded after dark.

The trouble begins at the assembly line. More than 10 percent of the energy used by a car over its lifetime comes from just making the car. That means a lot of heat-trapping carbon dioxide has been added to the air before even a drop of gasoline goes in the tank. Some car manufacturers are doing something about this. Instead of using oil to make the plastics for floor mats, car seats, and dashboards, they're using plants. That's right. Plant resins and fiber can be turned into plastic, too. And they're much cleaner. So much less carbon dioxide wafts into the air. Who knew the interior of a car could be made from corn, wheat, or soybeans? Maybe your first car will be a veggie mobile.

The Buzz on Travel

The megasized Dreamliner jet uses 20 percent less fuel than comparable commercial jets. It's made of lighter composite materials. Engineers even planned how the plane will be recycled when it reaches the end of its 30- to 40-year working life. A dream come true.

Keep on Truckin'

All over the world, trucks keep cargo moving. But they leave a trail of soot and other air pollutants. To deal with this problem, the Argonne National Laboratory in Illinois is working on preventing the release of soot from diesel engines by injecting air into the combustion chamber late in the fuel cycle. This gets rid of most soot particles without increasing nitrogen oxide, a key component of smog.

Green Home, Sweet Home

Home, Sweet Home has always been the American ideal. But now there's a new twist on it—our sweet homes need to be green. Tour this home of a family living the green life.

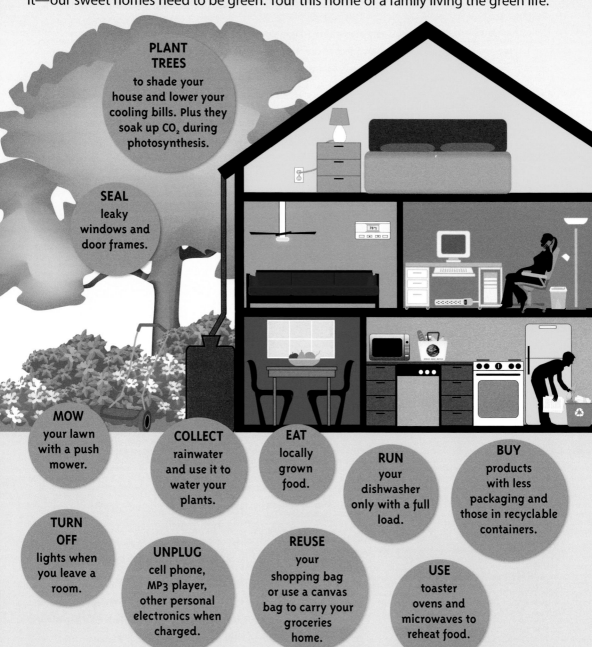

PLANT TREES to shade your house and lower your cooling bills. Plus they soak up CO_2 during photosynthesis.

SEAL leaky windows and door frames.

MOW your lawn with a push mower.

COLLECT rainwater and use it to water your plants.

EAT locally grown food.

RUN your dishwasher only with a full load.

BUY products with less packaging and those in recyclable containers.

TURN OFF lights when you leave a room.

UNPLUG cell phone, MP3 player, other personal electronics when charged.

REUSE your shopping bag or use a canvas bag to carry your groceries home.

USE toaster ovens and microwaves to reheat food.

Hello, Big Foot

The average U.S. home for two people adds a whopping 41,500 pounds (18,824 kilograms) of carbon dioxide and other greenhouse gases to the air every year! That's a big carbon footprint! Here's where it all comes from.

Source	Pounds CO_2
Cars	12,100
Heating/cooking	11,000
Electricity	16,290
Waste	2,020

How many kilograms for each source? Do the math to find out!

FIX toilet and faucet leaks.

TURN OFF the water when brushing your teeth.

SWITCH to clean energy. Tell your utility company you want to use power from renewable energy sources.

INSTALL low-flow toilets and shower heads and take shorter showers.

LOWER your thermostat in the winter by 2°F.

COMPOST your fruit and veggie scraps, coffee grounds, and use them to fertilize your plants.

RECYCLE paper, cans, glass, and plastic.

TRADE IN that gas guzzler for a more fuel-efficient car.

CARPOOL or ride your bike, hop the bus, or walk.

REPLACE conventional light bulbs with energy-efficient compact fluorescent bulbs.

UNPLUG TV, DVD player, computer, and other electronics when not in use or use a power strip.

LOWER your water heater temperature to 120°F. Insulate your water tank.

WASH full loads of clothes in cold water. Clean the dryer lint filter after every load.

[6] INDUSTRIAL WASTE NOT

Wrappers. Bags. Foam peanuts. Plastic bottles. Packaging like these overflow city landfills. Some industries are looking for ways to reduce their packaging. Others are trying to find more Earth-friendly materials to make them from. Check out what some industries and small businesses are doing for the health of our planet.

Ninety percent of floating ocean litter is plastic. See the yellow curtain? It's trapped all that trash so it doesn't go into the ocean.

Plastic Plague

The water that makes our planet a lovely blue from space has also been polluted. Rivers are choked with industrial waste. And you know where rivers eventually dump their loads. Plastic found in the stomachs of Antarctic seabirds shows that waste has invaded even the most remote regions on Earth. A giant mass of plastic trash, twice the size of Texas, swirls around the Pacific Ocean.

How Do They Know?

Don't Take It Personally, but Please Go Away

Chemists have invented plastics that break down in a matter of weeks, rather than the centuries (yes, centuries!) it takes regular plastic wraps to decompose. Demand in Europe and Asia for these packaging materials, which degrade in as little as 12 weeks, is growing at a rate of 30 percent a year. That's fast. Business is growing in North America, too, but not as fast because the new materials cost more. Scientists are working on ways to cut those costs, so we can stop worrying about plastic bottles winding up in the bellies of migrating whales.

Grabbing Some Rays

Okay, we know we can cut costs with solar panels on our homes, but what about industrial uses? In 2006, 700 kilowatts of solar panels were installed on a 32,516-square-meter (350,000-square-foot) building owned by the Port Authority of New York and New Jersey. Believed to be the world's largest solar array on a single building, the warehouse is used for food storage. All those solar panels not only cut energy costs, but cut carbon dioxide emissions—by a whopping 453,592 kilograms (1 million pounds)—in its first year of operation.

Experts Tell Us

Mahadev Raman

Building Physicist
Arup

When someone wants to build a library, a courthouse, or an office building in an eco-friendly way, Mahadev Raman is the person they visit. "We offer our customers a menu of options about how to do the right thing environmentally," he says. To cool the atrium of a Phoenix courthouse without air conditioning, Mahadev's firm devised an indoor mist system. Its fine droplets absorb heat and dry up before hitting the floor. And to keep a Massachusetts dormitory cool, Mahadev suggested concrete, which soaks up heat naturally. Mahadev's love of nature stems from growing up in rural Africa where his Indian parents were teachers. He used to bicycle to school through long bush grasses and watch wildlife. Today Mahadev is gratified to see more people becoming environmentally conscientious. "It's really nice to feel that there is a groundswell of interest in an area that you've been passionate about your whole life."

Ti-i-imber!

It's no joke. Some of the best timber in the world lies at the bottom of rivers, lakes, and seas. Some logs have been there since lumberjacks cleared much of the forest that covered the U.S. more than a century ago. Up to 15 percent of the forest logged a century ago sank to the bottom of rivers when it was sent to the lumber mills. These sinkers are being reclaimed by architects and builders who prize the denseness of the wood, as well as its rich color and textures. Other logs are part of whole forests that were submerged underwater when dams were built. These preserved trees are also eco-friendly lumber—no living tree has to be cut down for the wood. A remote-controlled lumberjack does the job. It's a chainsaw-toting submersible, named Sawfish (above), that dives deep to cut them down.

A Good News Story

The secret of making ink was known as early as 2500 BC, when the ancient Egyptians and Chinese learned to make it from berries, bark, and seeds. In modern times, people started using oil-based ink. Today, however, printers are using less polluting inks. Soy-based inks are now used by nine out of ten newspapers, from *The Los Angeles Times* to *USA Today*.

The Green Hotel

King-sized bed, cable TV, and room service. Isn't that what all travelers are looking for in a hotel? Surprise. Hotel operators say that many travelers choose their hotels because of their environmental practices. Some hotels use nontoxic cleaning supplies and in-room recycling bins. Some recycle water from the shower to flush the toilet. And some hotels run their front-desk computers on wind power. A few hotels are even planning on recapturing energy generated by the elevators stopping, the same way hybrid cars recycle energy generated by their brakes.

The Well-Traveled Tomato

The American system of food production is one of the world's marvels. But growing all that food uses a lot of energy. And shipping it to market uses almost as much. Some fruits and vegetables are trucked thousands of miles. The majority of food is carried on trucks, though that is nearly ten times more energy-intensive than moving food by train or barge. Refrigerated jumbo jets supply northern markets with produce from Chile, South Africa, and New Zealand, although that method uses 60 times the energy of ocean transport. That's why local farmers' markets are growing in popularity. Since 1994, the number of farmers' markets has more than doubled, from 1,755 to 4,400. So that's what those *buy local* signs mean.

The Incredible Shrinking Thermostat

Engineers are working to shrink climate control systems. They've developed a thin film that adheres teeny, tiny solar cells and heat pumps onto surfaces. Then the surface—say, a wall or a window—can use the Sun's energy to heat and cool itself. That could make heating and air-conditioning systems obsolete. And one day, your sodapop may be able to keep itself cool.

[7] YOUR TOWN

Throughout your state, across the country, and around the world, people are working to make their communities greener.

Growing Friendships

Ah, food from your own garden. Nothing tastes quite like it. Community gardens are springing up all over the country and they have many advantages. First, they produce food that doesn't have to be trucked in. They also help you get to know your neighbors, something too few of us spend time doing these days. Finally, they give the neighborhood another place for birds, bees, and people to gather.

Pool Pooling

To conserve water, Seattle has created public wading pools in parks all over the city. People are encouraged to use the wading pools instead of filling their home kiddie pools or running backyard sprinklers to stay cool in the summer. Want to cool your feet?

Now That's a Bright Idea

College campuses across the country are going green. Each of the 33 University of California and California State University campuses retrofitted their energy-sucking buildings so they can use energy-efficient compact fluorescent bulbs. The energy savings? More than 30 percent. That's enough electrical energy to power 2,800 homes. Hooray, they've graduated to green.

Grass Guzzlers

In fast-growing Las Vegas, the local water agency pays homeowners to rip up their lawns and replant them with desert-loving shrubs and flowers. They remove about 1,500 football fields' worth every year. This saves a tremendous amount of water since a section of lawn no bigger than a magazine page needs 178 liters (47 gallons) of water every year to stay green.

London Bridges Falling Silent

To reduce traffic, London, England, has imposed a fee of almost $16 a day to drive into the 26-square-kilometer (16-square-mile) central city. And it's working. The legendary traffic snarls that have afflicted commuters for years have been curbed. Singapore and Stockholm have imposed similar fees, with similarly encouraging results.

Hydro-a-Go-Go

During the 2006 Soccer World Cup, goals weren't the only thing being scored. Berlin's bus and subway systems tested two hydrogen-powered buses. Hydrogen produces no pollutants or greenhouse gases. Water is the only thing that comes out of the tailpipe. The hydrogen buses took thousands of fans from the airport to Olympic Stadium, where the final game was played. Germany is so high on the concept that the state-owned transport agency is ordering 250 hydrogen-powered buses. Soon, every fifth bus in Berlin will be powered by hydrogen. Go-o-al!

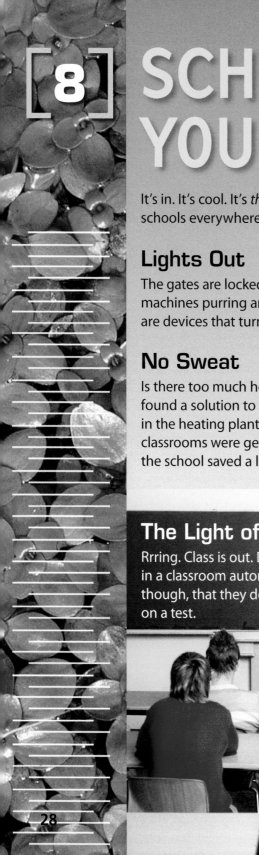

[8] SCHOOLING YOUR SCHOOL

It's in. It's cool. It's *the* thing on K-12 and college campuses. That's right, schools everywhere are going green. How about yours?

Lights Out

The gates are locked and no one's around. Except the vending machines purring and glowing like night-lights. Did you know there are devices that turn them off when school's out?

No Sweat

Is there too much hot air in your classroom? A high school in Canada found a solution to overheated classes. They contacted the technicians in the heating plant a few miles away who had no idea how hot classrooms were getting. The technicians turned down the heat and the school saved a lot of money.

The Light of Wisdom

Rrring. Class is out. Detectors can be installed to turn off the lights in a classroom automatically when no one is inside. Watch out, though, that they don't turn off when everyone is quietly working on a test.

Idling Is Wasteful, in Life and in Buses

It may be fun sometimes to just take it easy and let your mind wander. Letting the school bus idle, however, is bad for the environment. An idling bus uses a half-gallon of gas an hour. If you see your school buses just sitting with their motors running, you might tell the drivers that the Environmental Protection Agency's "Clean School Bus USA" campaign would rather they turn off the engines and breathe easy.

No Mo' Mowing

The grass may be greener, but it uses a lot of water. Try talking to your teacher or principal about replacing at least some of that thirsty grass around your school with native plants—plants adapted to the climate where you live. Not only would it save money and water, but your school will really stand out.

IT'S EASY LIVING GREEN

There are lots of things you can do at home, on your own, without joining a campaign or handing out fliers. And who knows, some people might see what you're doing and try it themselves.

Energy Pie

About a quarter of the energy used in American households goes into electricity for lighting and for powering our ever-growing army of appliances and electronics. Most of the rest—70 percent—is for heating and cooling. Want to reduce your energy bill? How about a sweater and an extra pair of socks? Cozy.

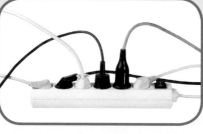

A Plug for Energy Savings

Did you know there are energy-stealing phantoms in your house right now? They sap electricity even when you're asleep. The electricity used simply when your appliances are connected to the power outlet is called the phantom load. These phantoms are definitely not friendly. They steal energy and money. A solution to the phantom load problem is to connect your appliances—but not the refrigerator!— to a power strip. When you go to bed at night, turn off the power strip. Sweet dreams.

Just Chillin'

That leaves the fridge. What if someone designed a refrigerator with a clear window and rotating trays with small doors like a vending machine? You could get what you needed without opening the big door and letting all that cold air out. Some manufacturers are working on this idea. Behind door number one . . . apples.

Tapping Water-Saving Ideas

Start with your lawn. Replace the grass with less-thirsty native plants. Save rainwater and use it to water your houseplants. In the shower, get wet, and then turn off the water. Soap up, and then turn on the water to rinse. Clean, smart, and water-wise. By the way, your teeth don't get any whiter by letting the tap run when you brush. Try wetting your brush, and then turning off the water while you buff those incisors and molars.

Going Gray

It's not only for oldsters. We don't need fresh, clean water for everything, do we? Gray water is water that's slightly used, maybe by washing vegetables or fruit. Try saving it and using it to water your plants. They won't know the difference, but your water supply will.

Sodapop Carpet

Plastic bottles have found new life in many homes as high-quality carpeting. No kidding. Carpeting made from recycled plastic bottles has several advantages over conventional carpet. The fibers are strong, stain-resistant, and come in rich colors. They also are competitively priced with nylon carpet. A step in the right direction.

Flip the Switch

What about the light bulb? Dad's right when he reminds you to turn off the light when you leave the room. But you're right, too, when you tell him to switch to compact fluorescent bulbs instead of incandescent ones. That saves even more money. Replacing one standard, 60-watt light bulb with a compact fluorescent bulb saves $7.48 a year—more than the cost of the fluorescent bulb. Plus, they last eight to ten times longer. That means fewer trips to the store to buy light bulbs, and fewer old bulbs cluttering up your local dump. It's a 2-fer.

Saving Fuel Can Be a Gas

If you are like most young Americans, you are probably on the go a lot. There are scout meetings, soccer practice, music classes, shopping at the mall, and on and on. You're in the car so much, you probably even wolf down a few meals there. Well, there are ways to cut the amount of gasoline being used by all these trips. You could convince your parents to combine trips. They might use a trip to practice to also go to the supermarket near the field, instead of going to their favorite store across town. Plan ahead and pile in.

Inflate Your Savings

Air saves money. Huh? Making sure the tires on your family car are inflated to the proper pressure can make a difference. Underinflated tires use 545 liters (144 gallons) of extra gas every year. And that's if you only drive 19,312 kilometers (12,000 miles). Most people these days drive more, sometimes a lot more. That's about $400 to $600 a year in money wasted.

Volts Wagons—The Hybrid Hope

If your family is in the market for a new car, you could help out by doing research on hybrids. These cars, which are growing rapidly in popularity, run on gasoline sometimes and electricity sometimes. Some of these cars get more than 50 miles to the gallon. In May 2007, Toyota hit the million mark in sales of the world's best-selling hybrid, the Prius.

You Can't Go Wrong If You Go Right

Do you know how much gas is wasted idling at an intersection waiting for a left turn? United Parcel Service does. The package delivery company developed a package flow software program that mapped out routes to avoid, including those requiring a lengthy wait for a left turn. In Washington, D.C., the program saved 193,056 liters (51,000 gallons) of fuel and cut carbon dioxide emissions by about 453,592 kilograms (1 million pounds) over an 18-month period. You might help your family and friends plan routes that avoid these time- and fuel-wasting delays. Right?

Don't Bag on Me

How many times have you heard a supermarket checker ask, "Paper or plastic?" Which is more "green"? Though both can be recycled, paper uses more water in production. Plastic is made from oil—and you know what that means . . . more carbon dioxide molecules wafting into the air. So what's the answer? How about neither? The best idea is to bring your own reusable cotton bag. Carry on.

Good for Presents, Not for the Planet

Unwrap. Unwrap. Unwrap. Avoid highly packaged food. All those juice boxes, plastic bottles, and paper containers add up to a big problem at the dump. They also require a lot of oil and water to make. Better to buy food in bulk and transfer it to containers at home. Cheaper, too.

Speaking of Cotton . . .

Make a fashion statement. Eco-clothing is finding a place on the racks of your favorite stores. Organically grown cotton is much more environmentally friendly than conventionally grown cotton, which requires a lot of pesticides. It also is an advantage over synthetics such as nylon, which is made from oil. Evening dresses made of old tire inner tubes? Belts and shoes made from tire treads? They're all leaving tracks on the fashion runway these days.

Friends Don't Let Friends Waste Energy

You're going to dinner with another family. Nobody knows where to go. How do you choose? Here are a few things to think about when planning your outing. Did you know the average food product is trucked 2,414 kilometers (1,500 miles) before you eat it? So you might choose a restaurant serving fresh items grown on nearby farms, rather than that fancy food shipped in from far away. Food with frequent flyer miles is a no-no.

What's the Beef?

Too much water. Water is used to grow or process nearly everything we eat. Bet you can't tell by looking at your lunch how much water went into making it. Take that burger, fries, and glass of milk—it soaks up almost 5,300 liters (1,400 gallons) of water! Meat by far uses more water than other kinds of food. Your burgie alone took 4,920 liters (1,300 gallons) of water to *grow*. You need water to grow the grains for the cow to eat, water for the cow to drink, and water to process the meat. Feel bloated?

35

Make an Eco-Wish

Okay, so it's your birthday. Congratulations, you're a year closer to getting your driver's license. How do you have a fun—and green—party? You could make your own invitations, using pictures from magazines. Serve organic food. Instead of wrapped presents, have your friends bring a plant or something they love and would like to pass on. And. . . many more!

4 u 2 Do

Change Your Behavior, Change the Planet

Try changing just one energy-wasting behavior for a week. See how it feels. You could try eating snacks that don't come in packages. Fruit could be a good alternative, especially if it is grown locally, since transporting food long distances by truck uses a lot of gasoline. If the clerk starts to put your purchase in a bag, you could say, "No, thanks."

Closing Our Eyes Won't Work

The problem is, too many people don't want to take the necessary actions to begin solving our environmental problems. Either they believe the dangers are being overhyped, or they think science and technology will come up with solutions, so they won't have to do anything different.

But the truth is, the solutions must come from us. And experts say the most important thing we must do is both really simple and really hard. Stop adding carbon dioxide and other heat-trapping gases to our air. Start taking better care of our precious resources—our air, water, land, and other living things. Let's all live in a way that lightens the burden we place on our Earth.

atmosphere (n.) A layer of gases surrounding a planet or moon, held in place by the force of gravity. (p. 8)

climate (n.) Prevailing weather conditions for an ecosystem, including temperature, humidity, wind speed, cloud cover, and rainfall. (p. 8, 29)

fossil fuel (n.) Nonrenewable energy resources such as coal, oil, and natural gas that are formed from the compression of plant and animal remains over hundreds of millions of years. (p. 9, 10, 12, 15)

gray water (n.) Water that is lightly used, such as water used to shower or to rinse vegetables. (p. 31)

greenhouse effect (n.) The warming that occurs when certain gases (greenhouse gases) are present in a planet's atmosphere. Visible light from the Sun penetrates the atmosphere of a planet and heats the ground. The warmed ground then radiates infrared radiation back toward space. If greenhouse gases are present, they absorb some of that radiation, trapping it and making the planet warmer than it otherwise would be. (p. 8)

greenhouse gases (n.) Gases such as carbon dioxide, water vapor, and methane that absorb infrared radiation. When these gases are present in a planet's atmosphere, they absorb some of the heat trying to escape the planet instead of letting it pass through the atmosphere, resulting in a greenhouse effect. (p. 15, 21, 27)

irrigation (n.) The process of watering fields to supplement natural precipitation. (p. 20)

photosynthesis (n.) Process by which plants use energy from sunlight to convert carbon dioxide and water into food (in the form of sugar). Oxygen is released in the process. (p. 17, 20)

phytoplankton (n.) Aquatic, free-floating, microscopic, photosynthetic organisms. (p. 17)

pollutant (n.) A substance that is added to the environment (air, water, soil) and can lead to harmful effects for living organisms. (p. 27)

Answers

4 U 2 Do Answer, page 13
As you pass the dark and light areas of the newspaper in front of the focal point the brightness changes. The dark areas absorb the light, while the light colored areas reflect it back. Parabolic mirrors can even be used to cook food or boil water.